# 100 Riddle Poems
# for Pocket Charts

## by Betsy Franco

Who's Down on the Farm?
Clippity clop, Clippity clop—
She lifts her head to neigh.
She's trotting to the big red barn
to eat some fresh-cut hay.
Who is she?

SCHOLASTIC
# PROFESSIONAL BOOKS

New York • Toronto • London • Auckland • Sydney
Mexico City • New Delhi • Hong Kong • Buenos Aires

## Dedication

*For Lauren and Andrew*

Cover design by Norma Ortiz
Cover artwork by Marta Avilés
Interior design by Sydney Wright
Interior artwork by Susan Calitri

ISBN: 0-439-25614-3

 # Contents

# Introduction

*100 Riddle Poems for Pocket Charts* provides you with riddles that are fun and educational. It also enables you to display the riddles on your pocket chart with picture cards that will delight your class. Having a pictorial, oral, and written answer to a rhyming riddle helps children make connections between oral and written language. It reinforces reading concepts for visual and auditory learners.

Activities in *100 Riddle Poems for Pocket Charts* show how riddles can provide a motivational text for teaching the following skills:

       ❋ letter and sound recognition       ❋ phonemic elements

       ❋ spelling and rhyming patterns      ❋ reading skills

       ❋ oral literacy       ❋ writing

Using all the elements of *100 Riddle Poems for Pocket Charts* will help you get the most out of your riddling time!

## How the Book Is Organized

*100 Riddle Poems for Pocket Charts* is organized into sets of riddles on a common theme. Each set begins with instructions for preparing the charts and developing a simple lead-in activity or discussion idea. These include book links, discussion topics, and list-making suggestions. Step-by-step instructions are provided for setting up and using each pocket chart riddle. To extend learning, activities are provided for each set of riddles. In many cases, these include one phonics-oriented activity and one writing activity.

Following the riddles are charming picture cards you can photocopy to enhance pocket chart learning. For example, in the section on *Who's Hatching?*, there are pictures for an egg and the animals that hatch from eggs. All pocket chart pictures can be enlarged to a size that works best for your pocket-chart needs. The pictures may then be colored and laminated for durability.

## Different Levels of Learning

*100 Riddle Poems for Pocket Charts* can easily be used with pre-emergent, emergent, and more fluent readers. For example, you can first read the riddle aloud, then have children chant the riddle with you several times. Finally, individual volunteers or small groups can recite it before the class. By reading the riddle aloud in a variety of ways, you will provide the repetition children need in order to memorize it.

The ways that picture card answers are used will depend on the level of the children. For young children, picture card answers can be lined up facing forward on the pocket chart. For older children, vary the setup—sometimes with possible answers in full view and sometimes with the answer facing backwards.

## Tips for Teaching Phonics and Building Literacy

A riddle can easily be used to help you teach phonics and build literacy. Try the following techniques:

✳ Children can hunt for words in a riddle that begin or end with a particular consonant sound. They can place sticky notes under words with the same initial consonants or onsets. For example, children could place sticky notes under all the words that begin with the letter *b* in this riddle about a community worker (p. 51):

> Let me help you
> find a <u>book</u>
> on <u>bears</u> or <u>bees</u>
> or how to cook.
> *Who am I?*
> **Answer: librarian**

✳ Some riddles include the first letter of the answer as a clue. These are perfect for beginning consonant study. The following riddle is about clothes children wear in different types of weather (p. 59):

> To keep my hands warm
> when building in snow,
> my m_____ go with me
> wherever I go.
> *What go with me?*
> **Answer: mittens**

✳ You can use a handmade or commercial "framer" to highlight words in the text that share a phonemic element.

✳ The rhyming words in the riddles are perfect for brainstorming banks of rhyming words. Children will also discover that rhyming words usually have a common phonogram or word family.

✳ In some riddles, such as the one below about a rain forest animal (p. 63), the answer rhymes with a word in the poem. A riddle like this can serve as a springboard for exploring words that rhyme with *fan*.

> With a giant-sized beak,
> and a tail like a fan,
> I've got bright-colored feathers.
> *I'm called a _____ .*
> **Answer: toucan**

✳ You can cover the rhyming word with a blank card and have children guess the mystery word.

✳ Some riddles feature a particular phonemic element, such as long *e* or the phonogram *-ake*. Children can find and highlight these elements by placing sticky notes under the appropriate words. For instance, words with the long *e* sound appear in this seasonal riddle (p. 73—in the words *trees, leaves, baby,* and *season*):

> In _____ time
> trees have brand new leaves,
> and baby birds fly in the sky.
> We like to dig and plant all day.
> We like the _____ time, you and I.
> *Which season?*
> **Answer: spring**

✳ Children can sort the picture cards into different categories. For example, the answers for the riddles about feelings (p. 19) are *happy, sad, angry, surprised,* and *scared.* These can be sorted by initial consonants, short vowel sounds, final vowel sounds, or inflectional endings.

> /s/s: sad, surprised, scared
> /a/a: happy, sad, angry
> /e/y: happy, angry
> -ed: surprised, scared

✳ Word walls or word banks may be used, and even illustrated, based on words in the riddle that have a common theme or a common phonemic element. An ABC word wall, for example, could be made using the names of the rain forest animals (p. 62).

✳ Invite children to choose the word card that contains the answer to a riddle. Have the class use phonics as they sound out the initial, medial, and final sounds of the words.

✳ Mix up sentence strips for each line of a familiar riddle. Then have children arrange them in sequential order.

## Tips for Using Riddles for Writing

Because riddles are simple and short, they are easy to adapt, personalize, and create.

✳ An existing riddle can be stripped to its skeleton and used as a frame for children to complete. For instance, children can write their own holiday riddles (p. 75) using the following frame.

> We _____ *[an activity associated with the holiday]*
> on this happy holiday.
> Can you guess the day I'm thinking of?
> *You're right. It's _____ Day.*

✻ Parts of a riddle can be covered and children can substitute new words. In this way, they can personalize the riddle, making it more meaningful. For example, most of the riddles about community workers can be rewritten like the following.

> Let me help you
> find a book
> on _____ or _____
> or how to cook.
> *Who am I?* _____
> **Answer: librarian**

✻ Children can write their own non-rhyming riddles on a particular theme, such as rain forest animals (p. 62). Results can be bound together in a collaborative class book.

✻ Children can complete and illustrate a frame based on a theme. For example, the following frame can be used with the riddles about the five senses (p. 21).

> I like to <u>pet my hamster</u> because <u>he is so soft</u>.

✻ The theme of the riddles can serve as a springboard for writing poetry or personal opinions in creative ways. For example, in response to the riddles about playing on the playground (p. 24), children can write inside of a ball shape.

"I really like to play soccer because I love to kick a ball."

## Tips for Promoting Oral Literacy

The pocket chart is perfect for shared, oral literacy.

✻ Children can chant the riddle together.

✻ Groups of children can stand in front of the class and recite the riddle.

✻ Individual volunteers might want to recite the riddle.

✻ The riddle can be read chorally with two different groups reading parts of the riddle, as with the following riddle about the five senses (p. 21).

> *Group one:*    A cricket does this with its leg.
> *Group two:*    I do it with my ears.
> *Group one:*    I do it when a siren sounds
> *Group two:*    or people scream and cheer.
> *All children:*    What do I do?
> **Answer: hear**

✻ Children can emphasize certain elements in a riddle when they read it aloud. For example, in the riddles about farm animals (p. 29), children can emphasize the sounds that the animals make.

❋ Some children could also recite the riddle while others act it out. The following seasonal riddle (p. 72) serves as a model.

In _____,

trees are orange and red,
*[children move arms like tree branches]*

and leaves are twirling in the sky.
[children twirl]

We like to jump in the leaves all day.
[children jump]

We like the _____, you and I.
*Which season?*
**Answer: autumn/fall**

## Tips for Promoting Comprehension

Riddles are perfect for promoting reading comprehension. In order to solve a riddle, children have to reread the text and find clues or details that lead them to the answer. You can assess children's understanding of the text by the reasonableness of their answers to the riddles.

Riddles presented in a pocket chart are beneficial and easy to use. They're short and sweet, they're fun and logical, and they promote literacy. Riddles also engage the reader on a visual and auditory level. Children will enjoy solving the riddles. And the pocket chart pictures will make riddling in your classroom especially fun!

# Which Mystery Color?

## Getting Ready

**1.** Copy each line of each riddle onto a sentence strip.

**2.** Enlarge the picture cards (pp. 13–14) on a photocopier. Then mount them on cardstock and cut out.

**3.** Color each crayon the appropriate color. You may want to laminate them for durability.

## Using the Riddles

**1.** Display one riddle on the sentence strips.

**2.** Place three or more of the picture card answers at the bottom of the pocket chart, or set the correct answer facing backwards.

**3.** Read aloud the riddle and/or have the children read it aloud in groups or as a class.

**4.** Invite a child to guess the answer by picking one of the crayon pictures and saying its name. Ask the child to support the correct answer with clues from the text.

**5.** Have the child put the correct answer beneath the last line of the riddle.

**6.** Reread the riddle and answer as a group.

## Going One Step Beyond

**Hidden Words** Once children are familiar with the riddle, cover all but the initial consonant letter of some of the words. Let children say the initial consonant sound and guess the hidden word. Then have a volunteer uncover the word and read it aloud.

**Color Lists** Use the images from the riddles and the books you have read to brainstorm a list of items that are associated with each color. Display the word banks you create on a bulletin board.

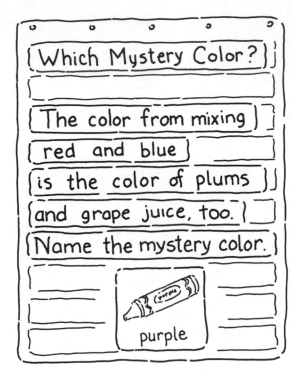

Which Mystery Color?

The color from mixing
red and blue
is the color of plums
and grape juice, too.
Name the mystery color.

purple

## Springboards

Read *The Color Box: A Book of Shapes* by Dayle Ann Dodds (Little, Brown & Co., 1992) or *Color* by Ruth Heller (Grosset & Dunlap, 1995). Ask children what their favorite colors are and make a tally chart.

# Which Mystery Color?

On American flags
both old and new,
there's red and there's white
and there's this color, too.
*Name the mystery color.*

_____

**Answer: blue**

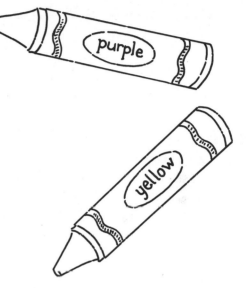

The color from mixing
red and blue
is the color of plums
and grape juice, too.
*Name the mystery color.*

_____

**Answer: purple**

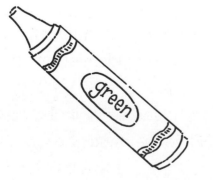

The color of a daffodil
that's growing in the sun,
or a bunch of eight bananas
that are ripening one by one.
*Name the mystery color.*

_____

**Answer: yellow**

Cherries, apples, pomegranates,
ladybugs, and roses.
At circus time, the clowns all wear
this color for their noses.
*Name the mystery color.*

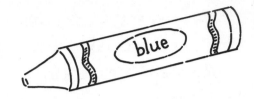

_____

**Answer: red**

The farm has rows of peas and beans,
some peppers and some lettuce.
This is the color that we eat
when Farmer Betty lets us.
*Name the mystery color.*

_____

**Answer: green**

It's a pumpkin in the autumn,
ripe and golden in the light.
It's a jack-o-lantern's face,
bright and scary in the night.
*Name the mystery color.*

_____

**Answer: orange**

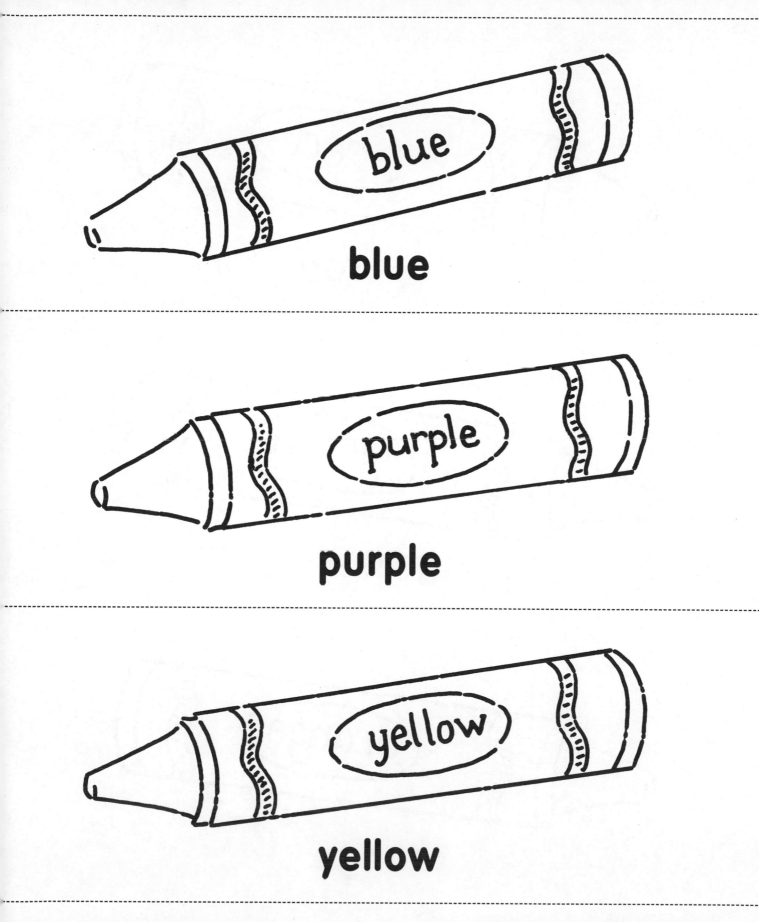

**blue**

**purple**

**yellow**

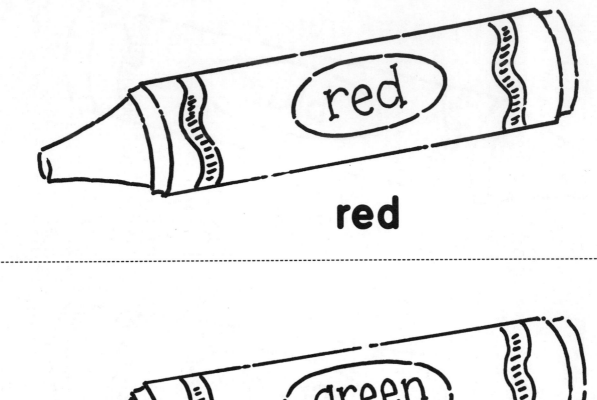

**red**

**green**

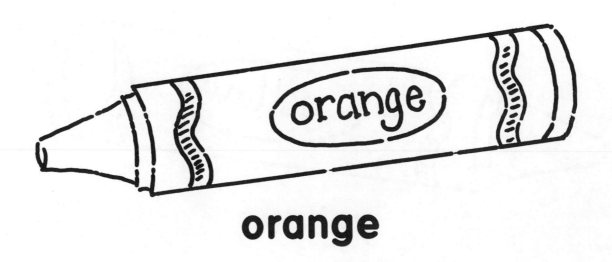

**orange**

# What Shape Am I?

## Getting Ready

**1.** Copy each line of each riddle onto a sentence strip.

**2.** Enlarge the picture cards (p. 17) on a photocopier. Then mount them on cardstock and cut out.

**3.** You may want to color the picture cards and laminate them for durability.

## Using the Riddles

**1.** Display one riddle on the sentence strips.

**2.** Place three or more of the picture card answers at the bottom of the pocket chart, or set the correct answer facing backwards.

**3.** Read the riddle aloud, and/or let the children read it aloud in groups or as a class.

**4.** Invite a child to guess the answer by picking one of the shapes and saying its name. Ask the child to support the correct answer with clues from the text.

**5.** Have the child put the correct answer beneath the last line of the riddle.

**6.** Reread the riddle and answer as a group.

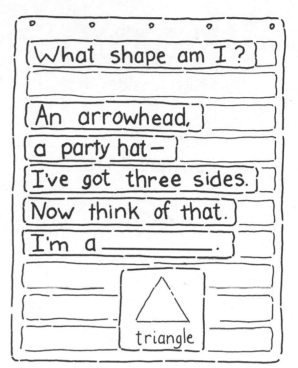

What shape am I ?

An arrowhead,
a party hat—
I've got three sides.
Now think of that.
I'm a _____.

triangle

## Going One Step Beyond

**Long Vowel Hunt** In the riddle about a square, have children place sticky notes below the words with the long *i* sound (*tile, sides*) and with long *a* sound (*game, same*). Ask children to identify the word pattern. (They each have a silent *e* at the end; they each follow the pattern *consonant, vowel, consonant, e.*)

**Writing More Shape Riddles** Individually or in pairs, let children make up new riddles for the geometric shapes. You may wish to use the following frame:

A _____ [Example: *teepee*]
and a _____ [Example: *slice of pizza*]
are the clues
I'll give to you.
To play this guessing game,
you say the shape's name.
Answer _____ [Example: *triangle*]

## Springboards

Read *Round Is a Mooncake* by Roseanne Thong (Chronicle Books, 2000) or *The Shape of Things* by Dayle Ann Dodds (Candlewick Press, 1996). Then, have children make a list of shapes they know and invite them to brainstorm objects that match those shapes. Begin the activity by having children look around the classroom and find objects such as the clock, for "circle", and a book for "rectangle".

# What Shape Am I?

A pizza, a clock,
a bicycle wheel—
I have no sides,
but I'm for real.
*I'm a* _____

**Answer: circle**

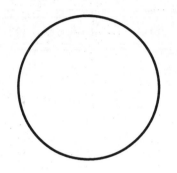

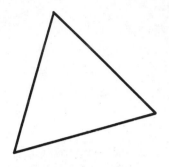

A door, a book,
a tabletop—
four corners wait
where my four sides stop.
*I'm a* _____

**Answer: rectangle**

An arrowhead,
a party hat—
I've got three sides.
Now think of that.
*I'm a* _____

**Answer: triangle**

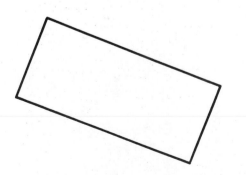

A bathroom tile,
a checkerboard game—
My four straight sides
are all the same!
*I'm a* _____

**Answer: square**

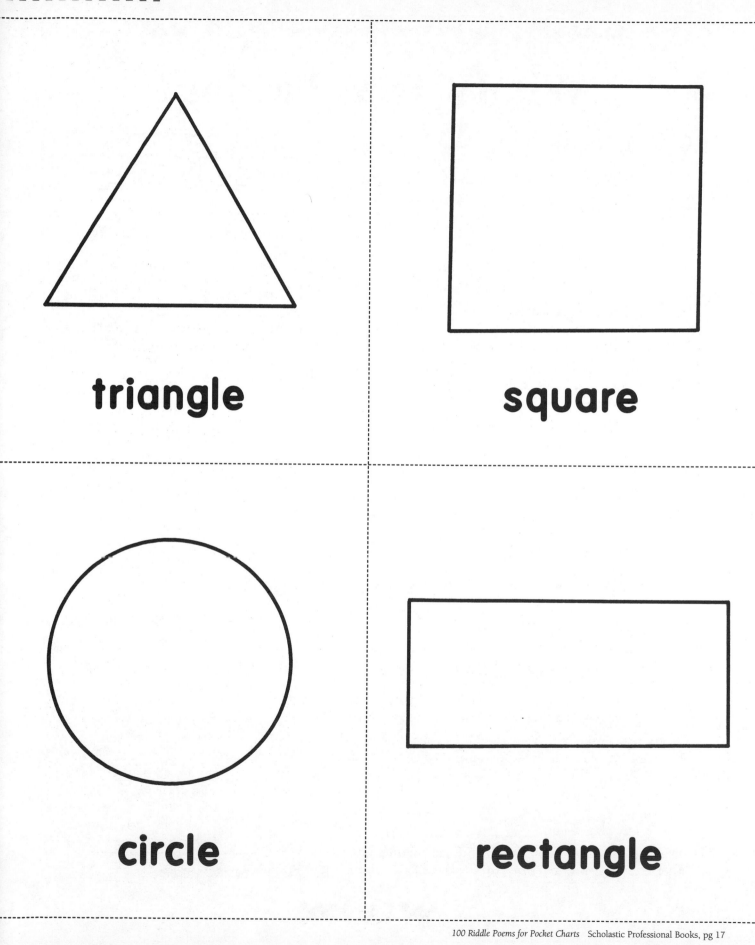

triangle

square

circle

rectangle

# What's That Feeling?

## Getting Ready

**1.** Copy each line of each riddle onto a sentence strip.

**2.** Enlarge the picture cards (p. 20) on a photocopier. Then mount them on cardstock and cut out.

**3.** You may want to color the picture cards and laminate them for durability.

## Using the Riddles

**1.** Display one riddle on the sentence strips.

**2.** Place three or more of the picture card answers at the bottom of the pocket chart, or set the correct answer facing backwards.

**3.** Read aloud the riddle and/or have the children read it aloud in groups or as a class.

**4.** Let a child guess the answer by picking the face that portrays the feeling and saying its name aloud. Ask the child to support the correct answer using clues from the riddle.

**5.** Have the child put the correct answer beneath the last line of the riddle.

**6.** Reread the riddle and answer as a group.

## Going One Step Beyond

**Sorting Out Feelings** Create word cards with the names of feelings. These can include *happy, sad, angry, surprised, scared, thankful, grumpy, silly, shocked, goofy, blue,* and *joyful.* Invite children to sort them into feelings that are happy and feelings that are not happy.

**Guess the Feeling** Give each child a paper folded in half. Have children draw themselves expressing an emotion on the front. On the inside, have them copy and complete the following frame.

> In this picture
> I am feeling _____ .
> I feel this way when _____ .

Display the cards on a bulletin board. Let children guess each other's feelings and then open up the cards to check their guesses.

## Springboards

Read *Lilly's Purple Plastic Purse* by Kevin Henkes (Greenwillow, 1996) or *Grandpa's Face* by Eloise Greenfield (Philomel Books, 1988) to introduce feelings. Invite children to brainstorm a list of feelings. Let volunteers describe a situation in which they had a strong feeling. Set a time limit for sharing.

# What's That Feeling?

Whenever it's my birthday,
or when Grandma brings us treats,
I get a _____ feeling
that's warm inside of me.
*How do I feel?* _____
**Answer: happy**

When someone breaks my favorite toy
or calls me yucky names,
then I feel very _____.
It's kind of like a flame.
*How do I feel?*_____
**Answer: angry**

On dark and windy Halloweens,
if someone yells out "boo,"
it makes me feel pretty _____.
Some masks have _____ me, too.
*How do I feel?* _____
**Answer: scared**

When someone hurts my feelings,
or a good friend moves away,
I start to feel pretty _____.
The world looks kind of gray.
*How do I feel?* _____
**Answer: sad**

**sad**

**angry**

**scared**

**happy**

# Which of the Five Senses?

## Getting Ready

1. Copy each line of each riddle onto a sentence strip.

2. Enlarge the picture cards (p. 23) on a photocopier. Then mount them on cardstock and cut out.

3. You may want to color the picture cards and laminate them for durability.

## Using the Riddles

1. Display one riddle on the sentence strips.

2. Place three or more of the picture card answers at the bottom of the pocket chart, or set the correct answer facing backwards.

3. Read the riddle aloud, and/or let the children read it aloud in groups or as a class.

4. Invite a child to guess the answer by picking the body part that is related to that sense and saying its name aloud.

5. Have the child put the correct picture card beneath the last line of the riddle.

6. Reread the riddle and answer as a group.

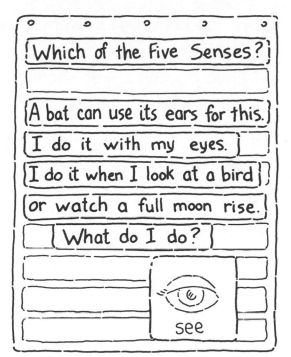

Which of the Five Senses?

A bat can use its ears for this.
I do it with my eyes.
I do it when I look at a bird
or watch a full moon rise.
What do I do?

see

## Going One Step Beyond

**Collaborative Book About the Senses** Have each child create a page for a collaborative class book about favorite smells, sights, tastes, sounds, and textures. Children can complete the following frame: *I like to _____ because _____ .* For example, *I like to touch my hamster because he's so soft.*

**Animal Senses** Have children mimic how each animal in a riddle uses an unusual body part to have a sensory experience. For example:

✳ A cricket hears with an organ in its front legs.

✳ Some bats have poor eyesight. To locate an insect to eat, a bat sends out noises. Then it listens for an echo bouncing off the insect.

✳ A boa constrictor smells with its tongue.

✳ A cat feels things with its whiskers.

✳ An eel tastes with its skin.

✳ A fly tastes with its feet.

## Springboards

Read *Busy Bunnies' Five Senses (Hello Science Reader! Level 1)* by Teddy Slater (Scholastic, 2000) or *My Five Senses* by Aliki (Ty Crowell Co., 1989) as an introduction to the five senses. Have children complete a table like the following showing the five senses and what part of the body is used for each.

| Sense | Part of Body |
|-------|--------------|
| seeing | eyes |

# Which of the Five Senses?

A cricket does this with its leg.
I do it with my ears.
I do it when a siren sounds
or people scream and cheer.
*What do I do?* _____

**Answer: hear**

A boa does this with its tongue,
I do it with my nose.
If someone's baking cookie dough,
then I am sure to know.
*What do I do?* _____

**Answer: smell**

A bat can use its ears for this.
I do it with my eyes.
I do it when I look at birds
or watch a full moon rise.
*What do I do?* _____

**Answer: see**

A cat has whiskers just for this.
I do it with my hands.
I do it when I pat a dog
or feel the silky sand.
*What do I do?* _____

**Answer: touch**

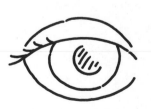

An eel does this with its skin,
a housefly with its feet.
I do this with my mouth each day
when I sit down to eat.
*What do I do?* _____
**Answer: taste**

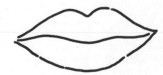

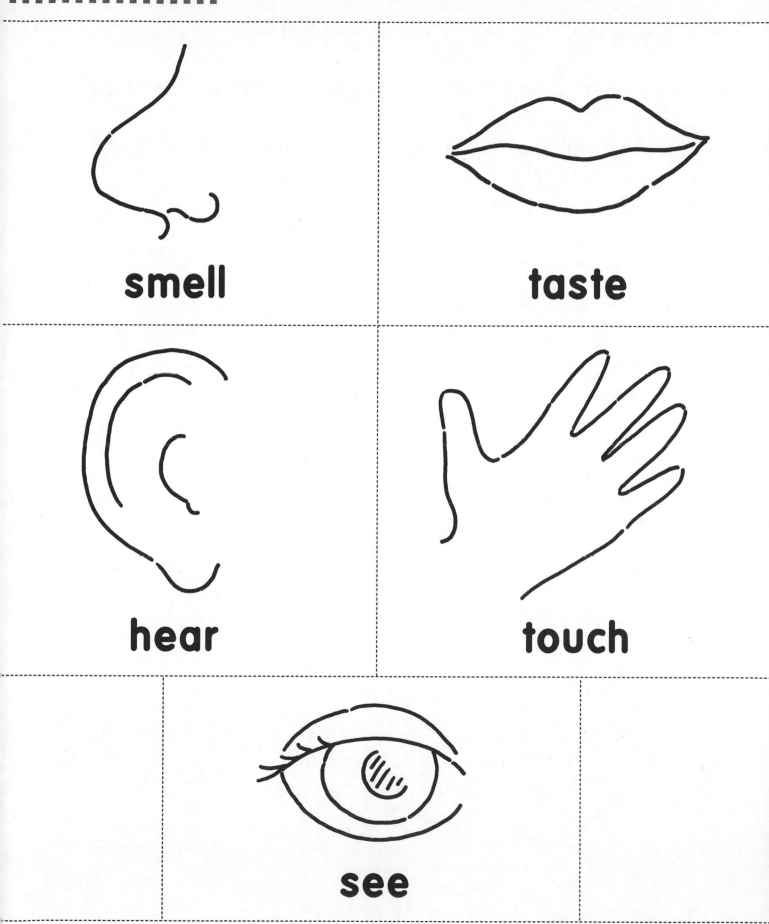

smell

taste

hear

touch

see

# On the Playground: What Am I Playing?

## Getting Ready

**1.** Copy each line of each riddle onto a sentence strip.

**2.** Enlarge the picture cards (pp. 27–28) on a photocopier. Then mount them on cardstock and cut out.

**3.** You may want to color the picture cards and laminate them for durability.

## Using the Riddles

**1.** Display one riddle on the sentence strips.

**2.** Place three or more of the picture card answers at the bottom of the pocket chart, or set the correct answer facing backwards.

**3.** Read aloud the riddle and/or have the children read it aloud in groups or as a class.

**4.** Let a child guess the answer by picking one of the pictures of playground equipment or games and saying its name. Ask the child to support the correct answer with clues from the text.

**5.** Have the child put the correct picture card beneath the last line of the riddle.

**6.** Reread the riddle and answer as a group.

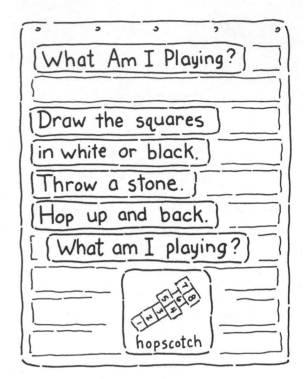

## Going One Step Beyond

**Opposites** When working with the riddles about the jump rope and the yo-yo, invite children to find the opposites in the poems. Brainstorm other words that are opposites. Have children make a two-sided display by choosing two words that are opposite in meaning and illustrating them on each side of an open folder.

**Favorite Sports** Encourage children to write about their favorite sports and why they like them. Their responses can be written inside an appropriate shape, such as a ball. Make a class book of the results.

## Springboards

Use the book *Playgrounds* by Gail Gibbons (Holiday House, 1985) and *Hopscotch Around the World* by Mary D. Lankford (Beech Tree Books, 1996) as a springboard into a discussion of playground activities. Help children create a web about the games and activities they engage in on the playground. Include the equipment needed for each activity.

# On the Playground: What Am I Playing?

Over my head
and under my feet,
the rope twirls around,
and I jump to the beat.
*What am I playing?* _____
**Answer: jump rope**

Its string is quite long.
It spins high and low.
It twirls up and down.
It's called a _____ .
*What am I playing?* _____
**Answer: yo-yo**

On my hips
it twirls round and round.
But when I get tired,
it falls to the ground.
*What am I playing?* _____
**Answer: Hula-Hoop**

*Swoosh!*
It's going through the hoop.
I make two points
and let out a whoop.
*What am I playing?* _____
**Answer: basketball**

Home run, single,
double, too.
I catch the ball
and throw it to you.
*What am I playing?* _____
**Answer: baseball or softball**

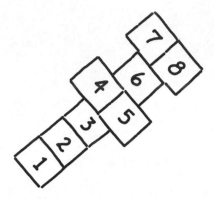

Draw the squares
in white or black.
Throw a stone.
Hop up and back.
*What am I playing?* _____
**Answer: hopscotch**

I kick the ball—
no hands, just feet.
Getting a goal
feels really neat!
*What am I playing?* _____
**Answer: soccer**

I'm "it." I chase you—
one, two, three.
I try to catch
the friends I see.
*What am I playing?* _____
**Answer: tag**

## baseball

## jump rope

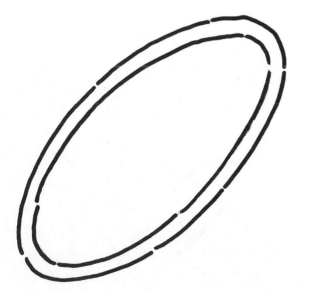

## Hoola-Hoop

## soccer ball

**basketball**

**tag**

**yo-yo**

**hopscotch**

# Who's on the Farm?

## Getting Ready

**1.** Copy each line of each riddle onto a sentence strip.

**2.** Enlarge the picture cards (pp. 32–34) on a photo-copier. Then mount them on cardstock and cut out.

**3.** You may want to color the picture cards and laminate them for durability.

## Using the Riddles

**1.** Display one riddle on the sentence strips.

**2.** Place the picture of the barn on the bottom of the pocket chart. Slip the correct picture card answer behind the barn.

**3.** Read aloud the riddle and/or have the children read it aloud in groups or as a class.

**4.** Let a child guess the answer and support the correct answer using clues from the riddle.

**5.** Invite the child to check the answer by finding the animal behind the barn.

**6.** Have the child put the answer beneath the last line of the riddle.

Note: For younger children, display the barn along with three or more picture cards. Have the child choose the correct picture card and place it on top of the barn.

**7.** Reread the riddle and answer as a group.

## Going One Step Beyond

**Animal ABCs** Working in small groups, have the children put word cards for the animal names in alphabetical order. For example, *cat, cow, dog, duck, horse, goose, owl, pig, rooster, sheep, turkey*. If children cannot alphabetize to the second letter, omit *cow* and *dog*.

**Sound Effects** Let children find the lines of the riddles that include sounds. Help children build oral literacy by having them recite the riddles with special emphasis on the animal sounds.

Who's on the Farm?

She chews her cud.

She softly moos.

Her fresh white milk's

her gift to you.

Who is she?

COW

## Springboards

Read one of Teri Sloat's *Farmer Brown* books, such as *Farmer Brown Goes Round and Round* (DK Publishing, 1999). You can also enjoy Bill Martin's *Chicken Chuck* (Winslow Press, 2000) together. Discuss the farm animals and the different sounds they make. Then, assign groups of children to a farm animal. Orchestrate a short concert by pointing at each group and having them mimic the animal's sound.

# Who's on the Farm?

He cock-a-doodles
on the farm.
He is the farmer's
loud alarm.
*Who is he?* _____
**Answer: rooster**

He has a very wobbly chin.
His wings flap up and down.
Thanksgiving Day, he'd fly away,
but he's stuck on the ground.
*Who is he?* _____
**Answer: turkey**

Her baby's called a little lamb.
Her coat is soft and white.
The farmer cuts her wool each year.
It keeps you warm at night!
*Who is she?* _____
**Answer: sheep**

She chews her cud.
She softly moos.
Her fresh white milk's
her gift to you.
*Who is she?* _____
**Answer: cow**

He barks and runs around a lot
to herd the sheep together.
He keeps the farmer company
in every kind of weather.
*Who is he?* _____
**Answer: dog or sheep dog**

He hoots and hoots in the barn at night.
He catches lots of little mice.
He turns his head this way and that
and blinks his two large eyes.
*Who is he?* _____
**Answer: owl or barn owl**

Paddle, paddle, paddle,
Dive, dive, dive,
Quack, quack, quack.
It's good to be alive!
*Who is she?* _____
**Answer: duck**

*Clippity clop, clippity clop—*
She lifts her head to neigh.
She's trotting to the big red barn
to eat some fresh-cut hay.
*Who is she?* _____
**Answer: horse**

**cow**

**rooster**

**duck**

**horse**

**owl**

**sheep**

**turkey**

**dog**

# barn

# Can You Bee a Bug Detective?

## Getting Ready

**1.** Copy each line of each riddle onto a sentence strip.

**2.** Enlarge the picture cards (pp. 38–40) on a photocopier. Then mount them on cardstock and cut out.

**3.** You may want to color the picture cards and laminate them for durability.

## Using the Riddles

**1.** Display one riddle on the sentence strips.

**2.** Place the leaf at the bottom of the pocket chart. Slip the correct picture card answer behind the leaf.

**3.** Read aloud the riddle and/or have the children read it aloud in groups or as a class.

**4.** Let a child guess the answer. Ask the child to support the answer by pointing to key words in the text.

**5.** Invite the child to check the answer behind the leaf.

**6.** Have the child put the answer beneath the last line of the riddle.

Note: For younger children, you can display the leaf along with three or more picture cards. A child can choose the correct picture card and place it on top of the leaf.

**7.** Reread the riddle and answer as a group.

## ☀ Going One Step Beyond

**A Good Time with Rhyme**  Cover one of the rhyming words in the riddle and have children guess the missing word. Once the word is revealed, invite children to brainstorm a list of words that rhyme with it.

**Bug Book**  Have children choose their favorite riddles to illustrate. You might instruct children to copy the riddle onto their pages before illustrating them. A collaborative class book can be made from the children's pages. You might also ask children to create their own unrhymed riddles about insects that weren't included on the riddle page. Let them refer to the list of bugs that the class brainstormed at the beginning of the lesson for ideas.

## Springboards

▪▪▪▪▪▪▪▪▪▪▪▪▪

Help children enter the world of bugs by reading *The Icky Bug Alphabet Book* by Jerry Pallotta (Charlesbridge Publishing, 1990) or *The Best Book of Bugs* by Claire Llewellyn (Larousse Kingfisher Chambers, 1998). Let children brainstorm a list of insects and spiders they've seen or heard about. Have each child describe one feature of each insect or spider.

# Can you Bee a Bug Detective?

I have 5 eyes,
2 pairs of wings,
3 body parts,
and other things.
But most of all,
I jump so far,
when it comes to my hop,
I'm a superstar.
*Bee a bug detective.* _____
**Answer: grasshopper**

I always wear a crimson coat
with dots on either side.
I fly away if I get scared.
It's hard for me to hide.
*Bee a bug detective.* _____
**Answer: ladybug**

Come to our house for the afternoon,
and help us make our honey.
We can pay you with a sticky treat,
because we have no money.
*Bee a bug detective.* _____
**Answer: bees**

I come from cocoons
so cozy and tight.
And when it gets dark,
I flutter near light.
*Bee a bug detective.* _____
**Answer: moth**

I have a lot of little feet
that I have never stopped to count.
They say I have 100 legs.
Now that is quite a large amount!
*Bee a bug detective.* _____
**Answer: centipede**

I spin a web.
I lay some eggs.
I walk around
on eight thin legs.
*Bee a bug detective.* _____
**Answer: spider**

My front and back look quite the same.
I wiggle all around.
You'll find me in the garden
digging tunnels underground.
*Bee a bug detective.* _____
**Answer: worm**

Children catch us
in their jars.
We blink on and off.
We flicker like stars.
*Bee a bug detective.* _____
**Answer: fireflies**

**moth**

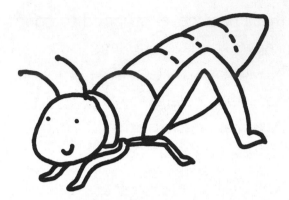

**grasshopper**

**ladybug**

**bees**

# Can You Bee a Bug Detective?

**fireflies**

**worm**

**spider**

**centipede**

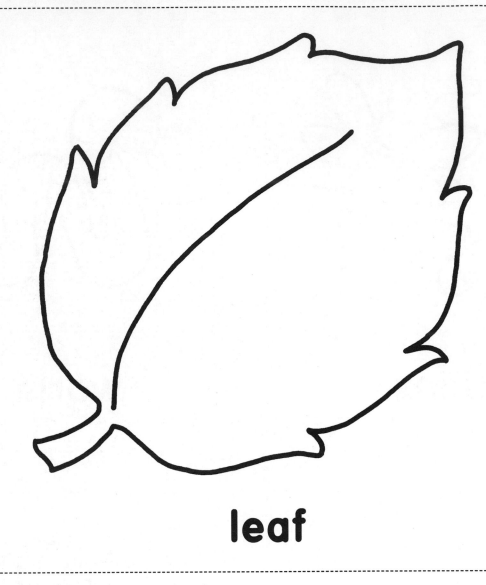

## leaf

# Who's Hatching?

## Getting Ready

**1.** Copy each line of each riddle onto a sentence strip.

**2.** Enlarge the picture cards (pp. 43–44) on a photo-copier. Then mount them on cardstock and cut out.

**3.** You may want to color the picture cards and laminate them for durability.

## Using the Riddles

**1.** Display one riddle on the sentence strips.

**2.** Place the egg at the bottom of the pocket chart. Slip the correct picture card answer behind the egg.

**3.** Read aloud the riddle and/or have the children read it aloud in groups or as a class.

**4.** Let a child guess the answer. Have the child support the answer by pointing to key words in the text.

**5.** Invite the child to check the answer by finding the animal behind the egg.

**6.** Have the child put the correct picture card beneath the last line of the riddle.

Note: For younger children, you can display the egg along with three or more picture cards. A child can choose the correct picture card and place it on top of the egg.

**7.** Reread the riddle and answer as a group.

## Going One Step Beyond

**Rhyme-Time Vowels**  For each riddle, have children place sticky notes under the rhyming words. In each case, let children identify the short or long vowel sound that is repeated to make the rhyme. Note that the riddle about the robin contains short *e* sounds. Children should highlight or point to each word that contains a short *e* sound.

**Do-It-Yourself Riddles**  Use the alligator poem as a springboard for children to become riddle writers. Individual children or pairs of children can choose an animal. They should give one clue and the initial letter of the animal's name to the class for the students to guess. For example, It has *a long neck* and it starts with the letter g.
**Answer: giraffe**

Who's Hatching?

A little baby's hatching out.
who's covered all in yellow.
He's peeping and he's cheeping.
He's a little feathered fellow.
Who's hatching?

chick

## Springboards

Read Ruth Heller's book *Chickens Aren't the Only Ones* (Grosset & Dunlap, 1981). This story will expand children's thinking about how animals are born. Use the information from the book to make and record a list of animals that hatch from eggs.

# Who's Hatching?

This reptile is breaking
her egg with a crack.
She hides in the shell
that she wears on her back.
*Who's hatching?* _____
**Answer: turtle**

They are skinny and long,
curled up in their eggs.
Then they slither right out
with no arms and no legs.
*Who's hatching?* _____
**Answer: snakes**

A little baby's hatching out
who's covered all in yellow.
He's peeping and he's cheeping.
He's a little feathered fellow.
*Who's hatching?* _____
**Answer: chick**

These creatures used to rule the earth.
They hatched from giant eggs.
They all had different sizes
for their tails and heads and legs.
*Who's hatching?* _____
**Answer: dinosaurs**

chick

dinosaur

turtle

snake

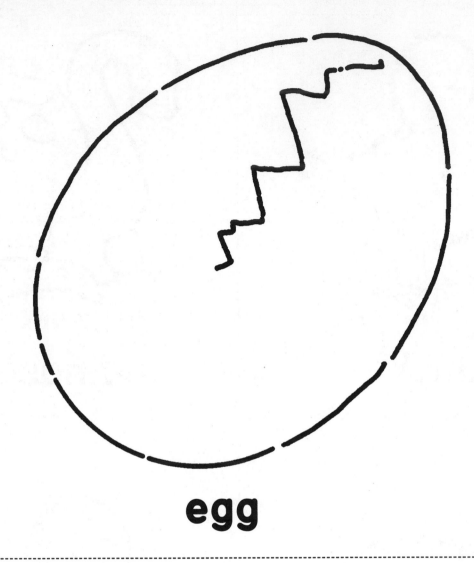

## egg

# Transportation: What Kind?

## Getting Ready

**1.** Copy each line of each riddle onto a sentence strip.

**2.** Enlarge the picture cards (pp. 49–50) on a photocopier. Then mount them on cardstock and cut out.

**3.** You may want to color the picture cards and laminate them for durability.

## Using the Riddles

**1.** Display one riddle on the sentence strips.

**2.** Place three or more of the picture card answers at the bottom of the pocket chart, or set the correct answer facing backwards.

**3.** Read aloud the riddle and/or have the children read it aloud in groups or as a class.

**4.** Let a child guess the answer by picking one of the transportation pictures and naming it. Ask the child to support the correct answer with clues from the text.

**5.** Ask the child to put the correct picture card beneath the last line of the riddle.

**6.** Reread the riddle and answer as a group.

## Going One Step Beyond

**Our Favorite Transportation** Invite children to draw a picture of themselves using a favorite form of transportation. (Note that it can be a form of transportation the child would like to ride in.) Have children write about why they like these particular forms of transportation. Create a collaborative class book.

**Let's Pretend** Encourage your students to use riddle poems as springboards for dramatic play. Children can act as if they are riding on a train, car, school bus, helicopter, rowboat, sailboat, or bicycle. You may wish to have a few students read the airplane poem aloud, for example, while the other children pretend they are passengers on a plane, flying high in the sky.

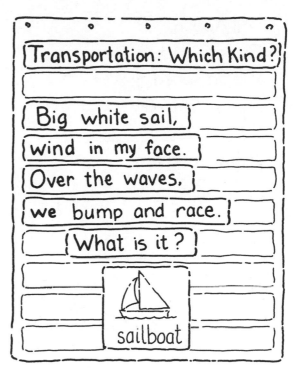

## Springboards

Introduce forms of transportation by reading *This Is the Way We Go to School* by Edith Baer (Scholastic, 1990) or *The Big Book of Things That Go* by Caroline Bingham (DK Publishing, 1994). After reading, make three webs that show transportation in the air, on the ground, and in the water. Discuss the forms of transportation children use to get to school. (Including feet!)

# Transportation: What Kind?

"All Aboard!"
Clackity-clack.
We go speeding
down the track.
*What is it?* _____
**Answer: train**

The pilot takes us
up so high—
a giant "bird"
up in the sky.
*What is it?* _____
**Answer: airplane**

With seat belts on,
we drive around.
We stop and go
all over town.
*What is it?* _____
**Answer: car**

Big yellow doors
swing open wide.
To get to school,
we ride inside.
*What is it?* _____
**Answer: school bus**

Up in the sky,
above the clouds,
propeller whirring,
fast and loud.
*What is it?* _____
**Answer: helicopter**

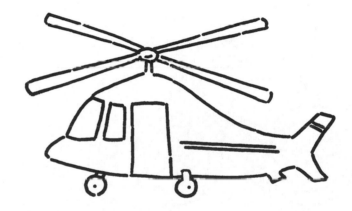

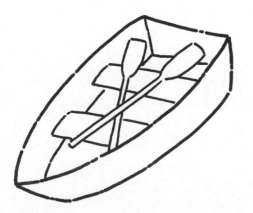

Across the lake
I row and row.
The harder I pull,
the faster I go.
*What is it?* _____
**Answer: rowboat**

# Transportation: What Kind?

Big white sail,
wind in my face.
Over the waves,
we bump and race.
*What is it?* _____
**Answer: sailboat**

Pedals twirl
and wheels turn.
We ride to school
and then return.
*What is it?* _____
**Answer: bicycle**

car

airplane

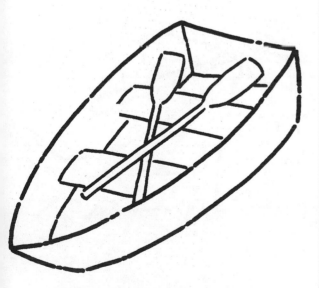

rowboat

train

## school bus

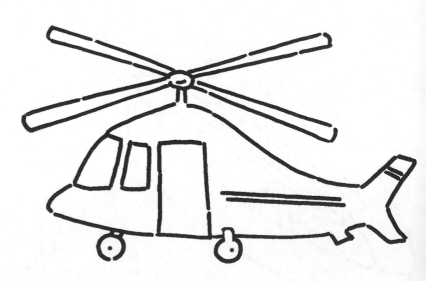

## bicycle

## sailboat

## helicopter

# Which Community Worker Am I?

## Getting Ready

**1.** Copy each line of each riddle onto a sentence strip.

**2.** Enlarge the picture cards (pp. 54–55) on a photocopier. Then mount them on cardstock and cut out.

**3.** You may want to color the picture cards and laminate them for durability.

## Using the Riddles

**1.** Display one riddle on the sentence strips.

**2.** Place three or more of the picture card answers at the bottom of the pocket chart, or set the correct answer facing backwards.

**3.** Read aloud the riddle and/or have the children read it aloud in groups or as a class.

**4.** Let a child guess the answer by picking one of the community workers' pictures and saying the name aloud. Ask the child to support the correct answer with clues from the text.

**5.** Ask the child to put the picture card beneath the last line of the riddle.

**6.** Reread the riddle and answer as a group.

## Going One Step Beyond

**Initial Sound Search** A number of the riddles have words that start with the same letter. (Sometimes that letter is part of a consonant cluster.) Children can place sticky notes under these words. Explain that this repetition of sounds (alliteration) makes the riddle more fun to read.

| | |
|---|---|
| Firefighter: | *fire, fire, fight, firefighter* |
| Doctor: | *stitches, slips* |
| Baker: | *cookies, cakes; bake, bread* |
| Librarian: | *book, bears, bees* |

## Springboards

▼▼▼▼▼▼▼▼▼▼▼▼▼▼▼▼

Read *All About Things People Do* by Melanie Rice (Doubleday, 1990). Talk with children about the community workers they know, starting with the school workers. Include people in service jobs or those who own businesses that serve your community.

# Which Community Worker Am I?

Fire! Fire!
9-1-1!
I fight the blaze
until it's done.
*Who am I?* _____
**Answer: firefighter**

Stitches and itches,
slips and falls,
colds and flu—
I fix them all.
*Who am I?* _____
**Answer: doctor**

In rain or snow
or sun or hail,
I walk to your homes
to deliver the mail.
*Who am I?* _____
**Answer: mail carrier**

I'm there for you
both night and day
so you are safe
at school and play.
*Who am I?* _____
**Answer: police officer**

I get up early,
just to bake
your cookies, rolls,
and bread and cake.
*Who am I?* _____

**Answer: baker**

You cross the street
when I tell you to.
When you're safely across,
I let the cars through.
*Who am I?* _____

**Answer: crossing guard**

Math and reading,
science, too.
I teach these things
to all of you.
*Who am I?* _____

**Answer: teacher**

Let me help you
find a book
on bears or bees
or how to cook.
*Who am I?* _____

**Answer: librarian**

**baker**

**doctor**

**firefighter**

**librarian**

## mail carrier

## police officer

## teacher

## crossing guard

# What's the Weather and What Will I Wear?

## Getting Ready

**1.** Copy each line of each riddle onto a sentence strip.

**2.** Enlarge the picture cards (pp. 60–61) on a photocopier. Then mount them on cardstock and cut out.

**3.** You may want to color the picture cards and laminate them for durability.

## Using the Riddles

**1.** Display one riddle on the sentence strips.

**2.** Place three or more of the picture card answers at the bottom of the pocket chart, or set the correct answer facing backwards.

**3.** Read aloud the riddle and/or have the children read it aloud in groups or as a class.

**4.** Let a child guess the answer by picking one of the picture cards and saying the name aloud. Ask the child to support the correct answer with clues from the text.

**5.** Ask the child to put the correct picture card beneath the last line of the riddle.

**6.** Reread the riddle and answer as a group.

## Going One Step Beyond

**Finding "-ing"** In the riddles about kinds of weather, the questions within the riddles include words with the inflectional ending -ing. On chart paper, keep a running list of words with inflectional ending -ing, for example, *falling, blowing, coming, floating, happening*.

**Consonant Clues** After children have solved all the riddles about clothing in different weather, make a new riddle by substituting the following onsets for those in the original riddles:

Replace *m_____* with *gl_____* for *gloves*.
Replace *r_____* with *j_____* for *jacket*.
Replace *h_____* with *c_____* for *cap*.

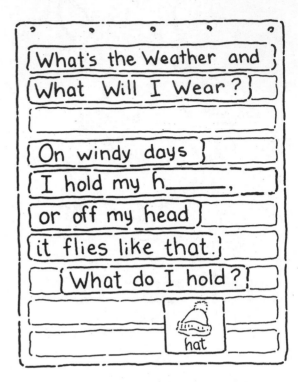

What's the Weather and
What Will I Wear?

On windy days
I hold my h_____,
or off my head
it flies like that.
What do I hold?

hat

## Springboards

Introduce the weather theme by reading *Cloudy Day, Sunny Day* by Donald Crews (Green Light Readers, 1999) or *Weather Words and What They Mean* by Gail Gibbons (Holiday House, 1990). Ask children to describe their favorite weather and explain why they like it. Have children vote on their favorites and record the results.

# Weather Riddles

In winter when it falls on you,
you always look surprised.
But when you try to catch the s_____,
it melts before your eyes.
*What's falling?*
**Answer: snow**

It can steal your hat.
It can blow your hair.
W_____ makes the leaves
dance here and there.
*What's blowing?*
**Answer: wind**

R_____ pitter-patters on the roof.
It waters garden flowers.
When we go out without our coats,
it gives us all a shower.
*What's coming down?*
**Answer: rain**

Small balls of ice
are falling down.
H_____ bounces up
when it hits the ground.
*What's coming down?*
**Answer: hail**

A zigzag flash
after RUMBLES and BOOMS!
There's th_____ and l_____
outside my room.
*What's happening?*
**Answer: thunder and lightning**

Puffy white pillows
fill the sky.
cl_____ hold the rain
way up so high.
*What's floating up there?*
**Answer: clouds**

When rain and sun
come out to play,
a r_____
colors the sky that day.
*What colors the sky?*
**Answer: rainbow**

It rises each morning and stays in the sky
till it's nighttime, and then it must go.
It shines on the flowers and gardens and trees
They need it in order to grow.
*What's shining?* _____
**Answer: sun**

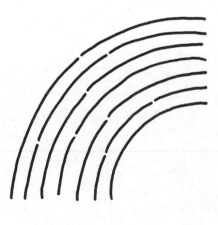

# Clothing Riddles

To keep my hands warm
when building in snow,
my m_____ go with me
wherever I go.
*What go with me?*
**Answer: mittens**

Whenever it's sunny,
I pull on my sh_____ .
I wear them to school
and for all kinds of sports.
*What do I put on?*
**Answer: shorts**

I put on my r_____
and pull on the hood.
Whenever it's raining,
my r_____ feels good.
*What do I put on?*
**Answer: raincoat**

On windy days
I hold my h_____ ,
or off my head
it flies like that.
*What do I hold?*
**Answer: hat**

**clouds**

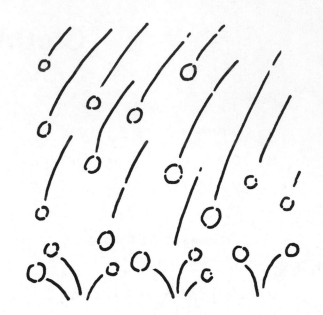

**hail**

**thunder and lightning**

**rain**

**snow**

**wind**

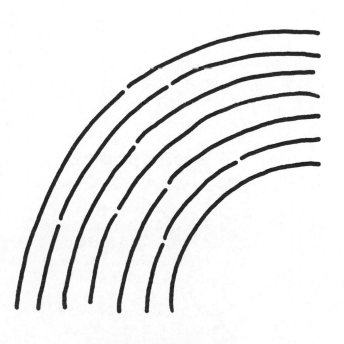

**rainbow**

**sun**

# Who's in the Rain Forest?

## Getting Ready

**1.** Copy each line of each riddle onto a sentence strip.

**2.** Enlarge the picture cards (pp. 65–66) on a photocopier. Then mount them on cardstock and cut out.

**3.** You may want to color the picture cards and laminate them for durability.

## Using the Riddles

**1.** Display one riddle on the sentence strips.

**2.** Place three or more of the picture card answers at the bottom of the pocket chart, or set the correct answer facing backwards.

**3.** Read aloud the riddle and/or have the children read it aloud in groups or as a class.

**4.** Let a child guess the answer by picking one of the rain forest animals and saying its name aloud. Ask the child to support the correct answer with clues from the text.

**5.** Ask the child to put the correct picture card beneath the last line of the riddle.

**6.** Reread the riddle and answer as a group.

## Going One Step Beyond

**Rain Forest ABC Word Wall** Start a word wall of rain forest animals. Use riddle answers and animals from rain forest books. Have children try to find one animal for each letter of the alphabet, and then display the words in alphabetical order.

**Riddle Writing** Have children write original riddles about other rain forest animals. The following frame can be used in which children pretend they are a rain forest animal and then give two clues to their identity. Remind children that the riddles don't need to rhyme.

I have _____

I _____

*Who am I?*

**Answer:** _____

### Springboards
▼▼▼▼▼▼▼▼▼▼▼▼▼▼▼▼

Read a book about rain forest animals, such as *Amazon A B C* by Kathy Darling (Lothrop Lee & Shepard, 1996) or *The Great Kapok Tree: A Tale of the Amazon Rain Forest* by Lynne Cherry (Harcourt Brace, 1990). These books will provide an introduction to or a review of rain forest animals.

# Who's in the Rain Forest?

When I'm eating my ants,
I couldn't be neater.
I use my long tongue.
*I'm a giant* _____ .
**Answer: anteater**

With a giant-sized beak,
and a tail like a fan,
I've got bright-colored feathers.
*I'm called a* _____ .
**Answer: toucan**

I have very long fur,
except on my nose.
I'm the slowest of beasts.
*I'm a* _____ *with three toes.*
**Answer: sloth**

Watch me swinging through the trees.
They say I'm very spunky.
See me hanging by my tail.
*I'm a forest spider* _____ .
**Answer: monkey**

I have two very bulgy eyes.
I live in trees and logs.
You see me hop, you hear me croak.
*I am a spotted _____ .*
**Answer: frog**

When I leave my cocoon,
I go fluttering by.
My wings are like jewels.
*I'm a _____ .*
**Answer: butterfly**

I am 15 feet long.
No sound do I make.
I've got a forked tongue.
*I'm an anaconda _____ .*
**Answer: snake**

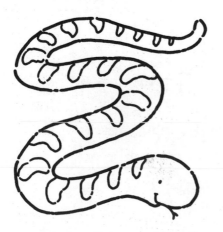

I'm fast and I'm sleek.
I'm a rain forest star.
My spots make me handsome.
*I'm called a _____ .*
**Answer: jaguar**

**anteater**

**butterfly**

**frog**

**jaguar**

**monkey**

**parrot**

**sloth**

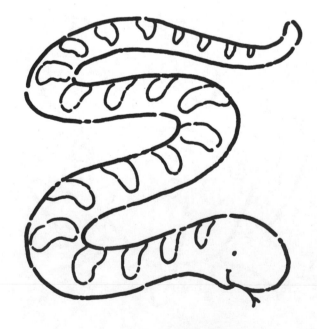

**snake**

# At the Beach and in the Ocean: What Am I?

## Getting Ready

**1.** Copy each line of each riddle onto a sentence strip.

**2.** Enlarge the picture cards (pp. 70–71) on a photocopier. Then mount them on cardstock and cut out.

**3.** You may want to color the picture cards and laminate them for durability.

**4.** Use a square of sandpaper to represent the sandy beach.

## Using the Riddles

**1.** Display one riddle on the sentence strips.

**2.** Place the sandpaper on the bottom of the pocket chart. Slip the correct answer picture card behind the sandpaper.

**3.** Read aloud the riddle and/or have the children read it aloud in groups or as a class.

**4.** Let a child guess the answer. Ask the child to support the answer by pointing to key words in the text.

**5.** Invite the child to check the answer by finding the sea animal behind the sandpaper.

**6.** Have the child put the answer beneath the last line of the riddle.

Note: For younger children, you can display the sandpaper along with three or more picture cards. A child can choose the correct picture card and place it on top of the sandpaper.

**7.** Reread the riddle and answer as a group.

## Going One Step Beyond

**Fun with Rhymes** Focus on the rhyming words in the riddles. Make a list from each riddle and add more words that rhyme with them to each list.

**Search and Sort** Invite children to sort pictures of ocean animals. The following are suggested ways to sort them:
* by size of animal
* by initial letter
* by number of letters in the name
* by number of words in the name (e.g. sea star is two words)

## Springboards

Use the book *Sea Squares* by Joy N. Hulme (Hyperion Press, 1993) or *Into the A, B, Sea: An Ocean Alphabet* by Deborah Lee Rose (Scholastic, 2000) to introduce animal life in the ocean. As a group, make a list of animals that live at the beach or in the ocean.

# At the Beach and in the Ocean: What Am I?

I look like a star,
but I'm not in the sky.
I cling to the rocks
when a wave comes by.
I'm a _____ .
**Answer: sea star/starfish**

You cannot spend me
at the store.
I'm a dollar you find
when you explore.
I'm a _____ .
**Answer: sand dollar**

Inside my shells
there is a pearl
for any lucky
boy or girl.
I'm an _____ .
**Answer: oyster**

Whenever I want to
switch my shell,
another's shell
will do quite well.
I'm a _____ .
**Answer: hermit crab**

I'm a fish with fins—
gray, white, or dark.
I've got rows of teeth.
*I'm an ocean* _____ .
**Answer: shark**

I squirt out my ink.
I'm a sourpuss.
I come with eight legs.
*I'm an* _____ .
**Answer: octopus**

My flippers help me
find a meal.
I swim and bark.
*I'm an ocean* _____ .
**Answer: seal**

If you're into large beaks,
then I'm the one.
I fish in the ocean.
*I'm a* _____ .
**Answer: pelican**

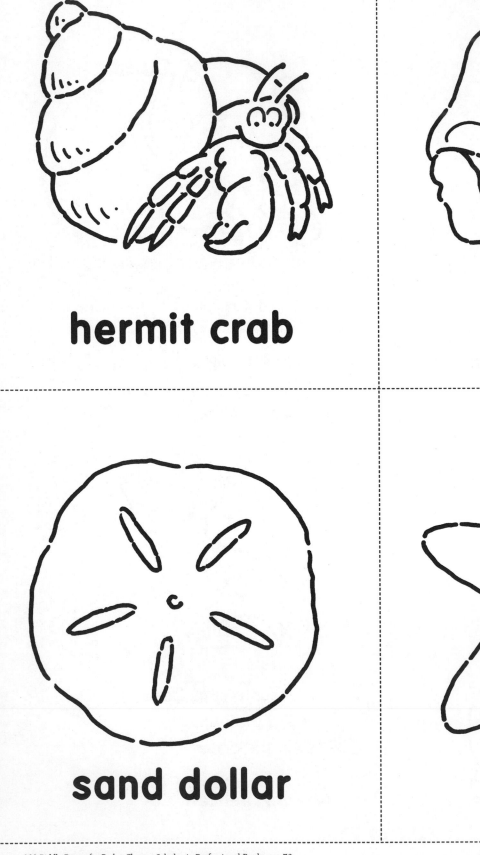

**hermit crab**

**oyster**

**sand dollar**

**starfish**

octopus

seal

pelican

shark

# Which Season?

## Getting Ready

**1.** Copy each line of each riddle onto a sentence strip.

**2.** Enlarge the picture cards (p. 74) on a photocopier. Then mount them on cardstock and cut out.

**3.** You may want to color the picture cards and laminate them for durability.

## Using the Riddles

**1.** Display one riddle on the sentence strips.

**2.** Place three or more of the picture card answers at the bottom of the pocket chart, or set the correct answer facing backwards.

**3.** Read aloud the riddle and/or have the children read it aloud in groups or as a class.

**4.** Let a child guess the answer by picking one of the trees and saying the name of the season aloud. Have the child support the correct answer with clues from the text.

**5.** Ask the child to put the correct picture card beneath the last line of the riddle.

**6.** Reread the riddle and answer as a group.

## Going One Step Beyond

**Trees with Leaves, and Other Long "E"s** The spring riddle includes words with the long *e* sound: *trees, leaves, season.* Place a sticky note under each of the words, and ask children to tell what is the same about all of them. Use the summer riddle to continue your study of the long *e* by highlighting the words *trees, green,* and *season.*

**Reciting and Acting** To promote oral literacy, assign groups of children a season. For each riddle, have the group stand in front of the class. A few of the members should act out the riddle while the others read it aloud.

## Springboards

Read *The Seasons of Arnold's Apple Tree* by Gail Gibbons (Harcourt Brace, 1984) or *Pieces: A Year in Poems & Quilts* by Anna Grossnickle Hines (Greenwillow, 2001). Then, create a web for each season. Include the names of activities and sights associated with each of the four seasons.

# Which Season?

In _____ ,
trees are nice and bare,
and pretty snowflakes fill the sky.
We like to build in the snow all day.
We like the _____ , you and I.
*Which season?*
**Answer: winter**

In _____
trees are full and green,
and bright hot sunshine fills the sky.
We like to swim and splash all day.
We like the _____ , you and I.
*Which season?*
**Answer: summer**

In _____time
trees have brand new leaves,
and baby birds fly in the sky.
We like to dig and plant all day.
We like the _____time, you and I.
*Which season?*
**Answer: spring**

In _____ ,
trees are orange and red,
and leaves are twirling in the sky.
We like to jump in the leaves all day.
We like the _____ , you and I.
*Which season?*
**Answer: autumn/fall**

## fall

## spring

## summer

## winter

# Which Holiday?

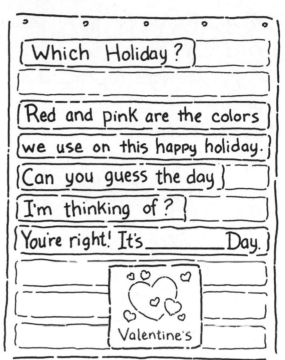

## Getting Ready

**1.** Copy each line of each riddle onto a sentence strip.

**2.** Enlarge the picture cards (pp. 78–79) on a photocopier. Then mount them on cardstock and cut out.

**3.** You may want to color the picture cards and laminate them for durability.

## Using the Riddles

**1.** Display one riddle on the sentence strips.

**2.** Place three or more of the picture card answers at the bottom of the pocket chart, or set the correct answer facing backwards.

**3.** Read aloud the riddle and/or have the children read it aloud in groups or as a class.

**4.** Let a child guess the answer by picking one of the holiday picture cards and saying the name of the holiday aloud. Have the child support the correct answer with clues from the text.

**5.** Ask the child to put the correct picture card beneath the last line of the riddle.

**6.** Reread the riddle and answer as a group.

## Going One Step Beyond

**Holiday Color Puzzles** Using the holiday colors from the riddles, split each word into two parts to create puzzle pieces for the children to match to form color words. For examples:

| p | ink |     | p | urple |     | br | own |     | gr | een |

**Other Holidays** Have pairs or groups of children create new riddles using the frame below for the following holidays: April Fool's Day, Mother's Day, Father's Day, Martin Luther King Day, May Day, Earth Day, Groundhog Day.

We _____ [Children write an activity that serves as a clue.] on this happy holiday.
Can you guess the day I'm thinking of?
You're right. It's _____ Day.

Let groups present their riddles and invite the class to guess the holidays.

## Springboards

Read *It's Pumpkin Time!* by Zoe Hall (Scholastic, 1994), *Thanksgiving* by Laura Alden (Children's Press, 1994), or *The Three Bears Holiday Rhyme Book* by Jane Yolen (Harcourt Brace, 1995). Brainstorm a list of holidays throughout the year, recording each holiday on a piece of paper. Let children identify the months in which the holidays fall and then put them in order by month.

# Which Holiday?

Black and orange are the colors we use
on this happy holiday.
Can you guess the day I'm thinking of?
*You're right! It's _____ Day.*
**Answer: Halloween**

Red and pink are the colors we use
on this happy holiday.
Can you guess the day I'm thinking of?
*You're right! It's _____ Day.*
**Answer: Valentine's**

Green and white are the colors we use
on this happy holiday.
Can you guess the day I'm thinking of?
*You're right! It's _____ Day.*
**Answer: St. Patrick's**

I make a present just for Mom
on this happy holiday.
Can you guess what day I'm thinking of?
*You're right! It's _____ Day.*
**Answer: Mother's Day**
(or substitute Dad for Mom. Then Father's Day is the answer.)

# Which Holiday?

Red, white, and blue
are the colors this day,
and there's a reason why.
Can you guess the day I'm thinking of?
*You're right! It's the _____ .*
**Answer: Fourth of July**

We throw up confetti
in all sorts of colors
on the year's first holiday.
Can you guess the day I'm thinking of?
*You're right! It's _____ Day.*
**Answer: New Year's**

Brown for turkey, yellow for corn
are the colors we see on this holiday.
Can you guess the day I'm thinking of?
*You're right! It is _____ Day.*
**Answer: Thanksgiving**

We celebrate Lincoln and Washington
on this very special day.
Can you guess what day I'm thinking of?
*You're right! It's _____ Day.*
**Answer: Presidents' Day**

# Fourth of July

# New Year's

# Halloween

# St. Patrick's

## Thanksgiving

## Valentine's

## Presidents' Day

## Mother's Day

# Notes